Easy Dip Recipes: Fast, Fun and Easy Gourmet Dips for All Occasions

Scarlett Aphra

Legal Disclaimer

CONNECT WITH US ON OUR SPECIAL FACEBOOK PAGE

Come join our Facebook page to be the first to hear when the next book in the Healthy Lifestyle Series is released. On this page, we will also share bonus content for you to enjoy.

It's also a great place to get any questions you have answered as well.

Come join us here on Facebook:
https://www.facebook.com/echobaybooks?fref=ts

Sign up for free ebooks

Echo Bay Books is proud to bring you our latest and greatest eBooks on Amazon. We treat you as a guest, and we treat our guests well. We promise to only send you notifications if it has some goodies attached that we think you will like. We launch our eBooks for free for the first 5 days every time. That means you will be the first to know when new books launch (once per week) - for FREE. No spam, ever. Just go to

http://bit.ly/1bMhUhf

to start receiving your free ebooks!

Table of Contents

Introduction

What is a dip? A dip can be a light lunch, appetizer, pretty dessert, snack and, of course, a delicious centerpiece for a casual or elegant social event. Dips are usually easy to prepare, can be served hot or cold and can be altered to conform to any diet or health concern. Dips can be cool, creamy, spicy, fresh, sweet, sticky, herb laced, cheesy and everything in between! Some dips can even double as delectable sauces for pasta or meat dishes if you happen to have some left over after filling your serving bowl. Discovering a signature dip recipe that delights your family and guests can be very satisfying and having a great collection of spectacular dip recipes on hand can be priceless for anyone who enjoys good food and entertaining.

<u>Dippers</u>

If you have a delicious dip you also obviously need something to dip into it. Some dips can be served with a dizzying array of products and other dips really shine with one simple dipper. An important consideration when planning your dip is what works best with a specific dip? Taste the dip with this question in mind and choose your dippers with care.

Foods that can be dipped include:
Vegetables- These can be raw, steamed, blanched, baked in the oven (potato wedges) and then cut into pieces or served whole (cherry tomatoes, green beans, baby carrots). Endive is also a wonderful dipping food because it is a handy scoop.
Fruits- These can be used whole (berries) or cut. Keep in mind that some cut fruit can be slippery, such as melon and mango, so little forks or toothpicks can come in handy. You might want to toss your cut fruit in a little lemon juice to keep it from browning, especially apple and pear wedges. You can also dip dried fruit into dips such as apricot, apple, peach, pineapple and banana chips.
Cookies- There is many options in the cookie aisle that work beautifully with dips. Some possible choices include graham crackers, shortbread, ginger snaps, macaroons, madeleine cookies, wafer cookies and biscotti.
Crackers and Crostini
Breads, Bread Sticks and Pita Bread- These are great cut into chunks and wedges.
Chips, Tortilla Chips and Pretzels

**Chicken Wings, Cold Shellfish and Meat Skewers
Marshmallows**

Tools for Making Dips

Dips are usually so simple that anyone can create them even with very little cooking experience. However, there are some tools or equipment that can be very handy when you want to whip up a batch of dip for a family get together or neighborhood potluck. You won`t need these items to prepare every dip but they can also be used for other culinary applications so why not have them on hand?

Food Processor or Blender: Lots of dips need to be smooth and the ingredients very well blended for the flavor and texture to be perfect. What could be easier than throwing all the ingredients into a processor and spooning out the finished dip a few minutes later? You don`t need an expensive commercial grade processor in your home kitchen so try and find a reasonably priced one that does the job.

Hand Beaters: If you don`t have a food processor a neat little electric beater can often be a good choice to combine ingredients in a dip. These are especially effective for cream cheese and yogurt based dips.

Chef Knives, Whisk, Wooden Spoons, Zesters, Peelers and Spatulas

An Assortment of Bowls

Measuring Cups and Measuring Spoons

Serving Dishes and Platters- A dip can be elevated to a work of art if you put it in the right bowl or arrange it on a lovely platter. Have a range of different dishes including heat proof ones to show off your gorgeous dips. You can get very creative with a dip presentation so look around your house for interesting food safe items that can be used for the dip or dippers.

Tips for Successful Dips

Dips often seem to fall into a more casual preparation area on the culinary scale but the correct combination of ingredients is still needed for a satisfying cohesive flavor profile. You can certainly just stir together a container of sour cream and soup mix but a truly spectacular dip needs a little more planning and care. There are a few simple things you can do to ensure your dips are delicious and consistent.

*A very basic rule to follow for any type of dish is: hot food should be served hot and cold food should be served cold. This also applies to dips. Hot dips should be served in thicker heat retaining crocks or even in a pretty functional fondue pot complete with tiny forks. A cold dip can be nestled in a bed of shaved or cracked ice. If you have a little time you can place a serving bowl into a larger bowl and then pour a little water in between the two and freeze it. No matter how you choose to address the temperature issue make sure it is an effective solution not just for aesthetic reasons but also for food safety. For example, cold dips containing mayonnaise or seafood should never get too warm or you can make people sick.

*Always season your dip with salt at the very end of the preparation otherwise you might end up adding too much. Many ingredients have their own saltiness which develops as the dip is whisked, puréed or sits for a little while. Once you add the salt you cannot remove it.

*Although dips are a very good way to clean out your fridge make sure you measure your ingredients carefully to avoid unpleasant combinations. If you are going to substitute an ingredient for health reasons, personal taste or to address a health concern consider carefully if other changes need to be made to make the dip work. For example, exchanging oil packed sundried tomatoes with water reconstituted ones will remove at least a tablespoon or more of oil from the recipe. You might have to add it back in to create the right texture.

*Cream cheese is often an ingredient in dips because of its creamy texture and pleasing mild tangy taste. There are many different types on the market so make sure you avoid the whipped varieties unless the recipe specifically calls for it because your measurements will be skewed. Most dip recipes call for room temperature cream cheese so plan ahead to let it soften. Do not microwave or melt the cheese because this will change the texture and ruin your dip.

*If you are having a very casual get together with family or enjoying a dip all by yourself it is okay to simply provide the dip and dippers. In most circumstances, it is prudent to provide small plates and a spoon for guests so they can scoop some dip onto their plate with an assortment of dippers. This is more hygienic and will eliminate the dreaded ``double dipping`` situation.

*Always use the highest quality freshest ingredients for your dip so the finished product is the best it can be and any leftovers will be usable. This is a great rule to follow with any culinary venture so you can take pride in the dishes you serve in your home.

Savory Dips

Yogurt Goat Cheese Dip

Most people don`t know that yogurt can be made into a very healthy tasty cheese by draining the liquid out of it with a strainer and some cheesecloth. This technique works very well with Greek style yogurt and the resulting cheese is fresh and perfect for delicious dips. This dip is absolutely gorgeous with vibrant reds, yellows and greens and wonderful for a summer evening on a patio or by a pool.

Ingredients
2 cups plain Greek yogurt
1 cup goat cheese, softened
1 Tbsp. minced garlic
2 Tbsps. minced red onion
1 Tbsp. chopped fresh basil
1 tsp. fresh lemon juice
Sea salt and fresh cracked pepper to taste
3 Tbsps. pomegranate seeds
1 Tbsp. chopped flat leaf parsley

Method
1. Place yogurt in a cheesecloth lined strainer over a bowl overnight to drain.
2. Transfer the yogurt cheese to a medium bowl and whisk in the goat cheese until smooth.
3. Add the garlic, red onion, basil and lemon juice and stir until well combined.
4. Season to taste and serve topped with pomegranate seeds and chopped parsley.
5. Serve with crackers, breads or fresh cut vegetables.

Guacamole

Everyone needs a tried and true guacamole recipe bursting with creamy avocado, citrus flavor and a touch of satisfying heat. This dip is better if you leave a little texture in it but that is a personal preference. Avocados are incredibly healthy for almost all the systems in the body and in particular, the cardiovascular system. It impacts the cardiovascular system by lowering blood cholesterol levels, regulating homocysteine levels (high levels are linked to increased risk of heart disease) and controlling blood pressure. You can adjust the heat in your guacamole by adding a little more jalapeno pepper and onion.

Ingredients
4 large ripe avocados, peeled and pitted
3 ripe red tomatoes, seeded and diced
2 small jalapeno peppers, seeded and chopped
1 small red onion, peeled and diced
1/2 cup fresh lime juice
1/4 cup chopped fresh coriander
2 Tbsps. real mayonnaise
Salt and fresh cracked black pepper

Method
1. In a large bowl mash up the avocado with a fork.
2. Add remaining ingredients, reserving some tomato for garnish, and mix until well combined. Season to taste.
3. Top with diced tomato and serve with tortilla chips or fresh vegetables.

Fresh Tomato Salsa

The trick to good salsa is fresh ingredients and the right balance of flavors. This recipe has very little added seasoning which allows the vegetables to shine and the colors to pop. Although the tomatoes are the stars of the salsa the peppers also add texture and many health benefits. One red or yellow pepper has almost double the daily requirement of vitamin C and jalapenos contain capsaicin which helps lower cholesterol. If you serve this dip with baked tortillas instead of fried it is a healthy delicious snack.

Directions

3 ripe red tomatoes, seeded and diced
1 small green pepper, seeded and diced finely
1 small red pepper, seeded and diced finely
1 jalapeno pepper, seeded and minced
1 small red onion, diced
 1/4 cup tomato purée
Juice and zest of 1 lime
2 Tbsps. chopped fresh coriander
1 Tbsp. extra virgin olive oil
Sea salt and fresh cracked pepper to taste

Method

1. In a large bowl combine all ingredients and toss to combine well.
2. Season to taste and serve with chips, tortillas or breads.

Traditional Hummus

Hummus is more than a dip; it is also a wonderful spread for vegetarian wraps and should be a staple in any household that tries to follow a healthy meal plan. Most people think the physical benefits of this creamy dip are from the chickpeas but another key ingredient is also packed with goodness. Tahini is made from ground sesame seeds and to get the full health impact try to purchase one made from unhulled seeds. This nutty toasty flavored paste is rich in protein, calcium, several B vitamins, vitamin E, phosphorus, potassium and iron. Use these recipe quantities as a guideline and feel free to adjust them to reflect your own taste preferences.

Ingredients
1 cup tahini
2 tsps. minced garlic
1/2 cup fresh lemon juice
1 cup water
5 cups chickpeas, rinsed and well drained
2 Tbsps. ground cumin
Sea salt and fresh cracked pepper
2 Tbsps. good quality olive oil
Chopped cilantro or paprika for garnish

Method
1. Combine tahini, garlic and lemon juice in a food processor and pulse until very smooth.
2. Add the water, chickpeas and cumin and process until very smooth, scraping down the sides at least once. Season to taste.
3. Transfer hummus to a serving bowl and drizzle with olive oil. Garnish and serve.
4. Serve hummus with pita bread, cut vegetables, breads or chips.

Artichoke and Roasted Red Pepper Dip

If you are looking for a rich mouth-watering dip look no further than this one for your snack needs. It is also delicious tossed in cold pasta salads and as a spread on sandwiches. All the ingredients are easy to find and it takes about 3 minutes to whip this dip together in a food processor. If you have the time try and roast your own red peppers for more depth of flavor, although store bought roasted peppers are a tasty convenience. For a healthier version of this dip you can reduce the amount of olive oil and use water reconstituted sundried tomatoes instead of oil packed.

Ingredients
1 1/2 cups artichoke hearts, drained well
1 1/2 cups roasted red pepper
1/2 cup sundried tomatoes
2 tsps. minced garlic
Juice and zest of 1 lemon
1 Tbsp. capers
1/2 cup chopped fresh basil
1/4 cup good quality olive oil
Sea salt and fresh cracked pepper
Chopped flat leaf parsley to garnish

Method
1. Place all ingredients except parsley in a food processor and pulse until combined but still chunky.
2. Transfer to a serving dish and top with parsley.
3. Serve cold or warm with cut vegetables, crackers, pita bread or chips.

Coconut Cashew Dip

This dip has an exotic taste that combines the complementary flavors of coconut, cashews, lime juice and a hint of complex heat. If you like hummus but want a little variety whip this dip together and enjoy! Cashew butter is a lovely alternative to peanut butter and is very heart healthy partially due to the fact it has one of the highest total antioxidant content among plant sources. Cashews are also an important source of copper and magnesium which is crucial for bone health, fighting anemia and combating weight gain.

Ingredients
1 cup chickpeas, rinsed and drained
1/2 cup coconut milk
1/2 cup cashew butter
2 Tbsps. lime juice
1 tsp. low-sodium soy sauce
1 tsp. brown sugar
1 tsp. rice vinegar
1/2 tsp. chili paste
Sea salt to taste
Chopped cashews

Method
1. Combine all ingredients except chopped cashews in a food processor until well combined and smooth.
2. Transfer to a serving dish and top with chopped cashews.
3. Store in fridge at least an hour to let flavors mellow and serve with crackers, vegetables, pita bread or chips.

Creamy Salmon Dip with Horseradish

Smoked salmon has an undeniably decadent flavor, even in small quantities, which hints of a naughty indulgence. The richness of this easy smoked salmon dip makes it seems like it should be consumed accompanied by a glass of champagne on the deck of a yacht. If you don't have a yacht or it is too early for champagne try it instead as a tasty brunch treat and perfect late afternoon treat with lightly toasted bread or crackers. Always look for wild caught smoked salmon because there is less chance of the harmful toxins sometimes found in the farm raised counterparts. Despite its richness smoked salmon is low in fat and a good source of protein, vitamin D and selenium. If you want to create an even healthier dip simply use light cream cheese instead of the full fat version.

Ingredients

2 cups plain cream cheese, at room temperature
1 small red pepper, seeded and diced
1 small yellow pepper, seeded and chopped
3 Tbsps. chopped scallion
3 Tbsps. chopped cucumber
2 Tbsps. prepared horseradish
2 Tbsps. chopped fresh dill
2 Tbsps. fresh lemon juice
11/2 cups chopped smoked salmon
Sea salt and black pepper

Method

1. In a medium bowl beat cream cheese until it is very smooth, scraping down the sides of the bowl.
2. Stir in the remaining ingredients until well combined and season to taste.
3. Chill in the dip in the fridge until ready to serve.
4. Serve with the crackers or fresh cut vegetables.

Blue Cheese Dip

Blue cheese dip is a required accompaniment for chicken wings in many countries around the world. There is something incredible about its cool creamy tanginess combined with a hot sauced meaty wingette or drumette. This dip is not traditionally very healthy but it can be lightened up to create a result that doesn't require a defibrillator at the table. Use fat free and light versions of sour cream and mayonnaise as the base and reduce the amount of blue cheese if you are really concerned about calories or fat. There are also lower fat blue cheeses available as well but they do not have that satisfying tangy taste which is the main reason these cheeses are coveted.

Ingredients

1 cup fat free sour cream or light plain yogurt
1/2 cup soft goat cheese
1 cup light mayonnaise
1/2 cup chopped green onion
1 cup crumbled blue cheese
Sea salt and fresh cracked black pepper

Method

1. Whisk together sour cream, goat cheese and mayonnaise until well combined. It is okay if it is not completely smooth.
2. Stir in green onion and blue cheese.
3. Season to taste.
4. Serve with cut vegetables, crackers and chicken wings.

Melon Pico de Gallo

Salsa aficionados will absolutely love this stunning pastel creation because it is everything a good salsa should be: fresh, fragrant, crunchy and a hint of heat. Melon is a wonderful addition to savory dishes because it has a robust crunchy texture and sweet almost squash like flavor that combines well with vegetables and spice. If you want to create a less sweet salsa use a honeydew melon that is slightly under ripe. Melons are extremely low in fat and calories and high in many important vitamins and minerals such as vitamin C, vitamin A and potassium. This salsa is also lovely with chopped basil or cilantro if thyme is not your favorite herb.

Ingredients
1/4 small seedless yellow watermelon, diced small
1/4 small honeydew melon, diced small
1 small English cucumber, peeled and diced small
1/4 cup chopped scallion
2 Tbsps. fresh lime juice
1 tsp. chopped fresh thyme
1/4 tsp. grated fresh ginger
Sea salt and black pepper

Method
1. In a medium bowl, combine all ingredients until well combined. Season to taste.
2. Serve with tortilla chips or pita bread.

Fresh Corn and Green Chile Salsa

This salsa is fabulous as is but for a truly amazing culinary experience take the time to grill your corn on a BBQ before removing the kernels. Simply soak the corn in water, right in the husks, and place on a preheated BBQ until the kernels are smoky and tender. Corn pairs perfectly with the tomatoes, jalapeno and cool cucumber so continue the theme and serve this vibrant salsa with corn tortillas. This is really a summer dish that is best when you use fresh in season corn cobs ideally purchased at a bustling farmers market or roadside stand. Corn is a great source of antioxidants and fiber which promotes good health while you enjoy the dip.

Ingredients
2 ears fresh corn, kernels removed
2 large tomatoes, seeded and diced
1 small yellow pepper, seeded and diced
1/2 cup chopped cucumber
1/2 cup chopped green chilies
1/2 cup chopped scallion
Juice of 1 lime
1 tsp. cumin
1/2 tsp. coriander
Sea salt and fresh cracked pepper to taste
Red chili flakes (optional)

Method
1. In a medium bowl combine all ingredients until well mixed and adjust seasoning.
2. Serve chilled with tortilla chips.

Spicy Crab Dip

Sometimes familiar dips will simply not satisfy your cravings and a different taste is needed for an event. A crab dip is usually a popular addition for any gathering because the sweet taste of crab combines perfectly with citrus, creamy cheese and the heat of chili sauce while seeming like an exotic treat. Crab is a nice choice for dips because it is low in fat but a great source of heart-healthy omega-3 fatty acids. However, if you are on a sodium restricted diet you might want to steer clear of this dip because crabs are high in natural sodium.

Ingredients

1 cup plain cream cheese, at room temperature
1 small red pepper, seeded and minced
3/4 cup crab meat
1/2 cup chili sauce
2 Tbsps. fresh lemon juice
2 Tbsps. minced sweet onion
1 Tbsp. Worcestershire sauce

Method

1. Combine all ingredients in a medium bowl until very well mixed.
2. Transfer to a serving dish and store in the fridge until you are ready to serve the dip.
3. Serve hot or chilled with crackers, breads or cut vegetables.

Baba Ghanouj

This dip is a staple in most vegetarian cuisine devoted fridges because it is so versatile and delicious. It can be used as a lovely dip, tossed in whole wheat pasta, eaten spread on sandwiches or wraps and as a topping for rice or couscous. Make sure you take the time to roast your eggplants well to remove any of the characteristic bitterness associated with this nightshade vegetable. Eggplant has many health benefits such as supporting good cardiovascular and brain health and its spongy texture is perfect for soaking up flavor. However, people with existing gallbladder or kidney issues should avoid eggplant due to this vegetable`s oxalate content.

Ingredients

2 medium eggplants
3/4 cup tahini
1/2 cup lemon juice
2 tsps. minced garlic
Sea salt and pepper
1 small red onion, chopped
2 large ripe tomatoes, seeded and finely chopped
1/2 cup chopped fresh parsley
3 Tbsps. good quality olive oil

Method

1. Preheat oven to 350 degrees F. and oil a baking sheet lined with foil.
2. Place whole eggplants the baking sheet and roast turning occasionally until the flesh is soft, about an hour. Remove from oven and let stand until cool enough to handle.
3. Peel the skin from the eggplants and transfer the pulp to a food processor and pulse until smooth.
4. Add the tahini, lemon juice and garlic and process until smooth.
5. Transfer eggplant mixture to a medium bowl and season to taste.
6. Add onion, tomatoes, parsley and oil. Stir to combine well and place in the fridge for at least an hour before serving.
7. Serve chilled or warm with chips, baguette slices or pita bread.

Roasted Red Pepper Dip

This dip contains an entire head of garlic which might scare some people off. Don`t be frightened though because the garlic is roasted to a mellow flavored creamy consistency that is pleasing on the tongue and won`t repel people who want to get close to you! Roasting garlic is as simple as cutting the top off the garlic clove, applying a generous coat of olive oil and popping it in a moderate oven for about 45 minutes. Garlic is a member of the lily family and the subject of countless books devoted to the health benefits of this lovely bulb. It benefits the cardiovascular system, musculoskeletal system, respiratory system and digestive system. This dip would make a healthy addition to snacks, light lunches and even tossed into whole wheat pasta as a sauce.

Ingredients

4 whole roasted red peppers, seeded, skin removed and chopped
1 small red pepper, seeded and chopped
2 ripe tomatoes, seeded and chopped
1 whole head of roasted garlic, pulp squeezed out
1 cup soft goat cheese
2 Tbsps. good quality olive oil
1/2 cup chopped fresh basil
Cayenne pepper to taste
Sea salt and fresh cracked pepper

Method

1. In a large bowl combine all ingredients until very well mixed.
2. Transfer dip to serving bowl and place in the fridge for at least an hour to let flavors mellow.
3. Serve with fresh cut vegetables, crackers, breads or tortilla chips.

Curried Lentil Dip

This dip has a satisfying texture as well as a complex taste and you might find yourself eating it with a spoon instead of dipping a cracker in it! Yellow lentils are easy to find, both canned and dry, in most supermarkets as are red and green lentils. You can use any kind for this recipe or combine them for an interesting look. Lentils are nutrient packed pulses that are valuable for weight loss, stabilizing blood sugar, cardiovascular health and preventing several kinds of cancer. You can adjust the heat of this dip by using hot curry paste instead of mild and including a touch of cayenne.

Ingredient

1 tsp. extra virgin olive oil
1 cup diced sweet onion
2 tsps. minced garlic
3 cups cooked yellow lentils, rinsed and drained
1/2 cup toasted sunflower seeds
1/2 cup golden raisins
1/4 cup coconut milk
2 Tbsps. lime juice
2 tsps. mild curry paste
1 tsp. garam masala
1/2 tsp. cumin
Sea salt and cracked black pepper

Method

1. Heat oil in a small skillet over medium low heat and sauté the onion and garlic until translucent.
2. Add the rest of the ingredients and simmer until the flavors are well combined, about 10 minutes.
3. Spoon lentil mixture into a serving dish and place in the fridge until you are ready to serve it.
4. Serve with tortilla chips, pita bread or crackers either cool or at room temperature.

Sour Cream Onion Dip

Onion dip is one of those chip accompaniments that most people remember from their childhood although that dip was usually sour cream mixed with a little dried onion soup mix. This fresh made version is better and features sautéed onions, creamy yogurt and the satisfying bite of a fresh squeezed lemon. The trick to an incredible onion dip lies in carefully, patiently caramelizing the onions. If your onions are very young and juicy you might have to add a little more sugar to speed up this process. You can create a healthier dip by using light yogurt and eliminating the soy sauce.

Ingredients
1 cup plain Greek yogurt
1/3 cup good quality olive oil
2 cups diced sweet onion
1 tsp. granulated sugar
1 Tbsp. fresh lemon juice
1 tsp. low sodium soy sauce
1/3 cup fat free sour cream
Sea salt and cracked black pepper
3 tsps. chopped chives

Method
1. Place yogurt in a cheesecloth lined strainer over a bowl overnight to drain.
2. Transfer the yogurt cheese to a medium bowl and set aside.
3. Place a large skillet over medium low heat and add olive oil. Sauté onions in hot oil with the sugar until caramelized, about 20 minutes.
4. Remove from heat and stir onions into yogurt cheese. Add remaining ingredients except chives and stir until well combined.
5. Top with chives and refrigerate until cold.
6. Serve with chips.

Sundried Tomato Dip

Do not be surprised if you find yourself sitting at your kitchen table eating this dip with a spoon and hiding the container in the fridge to hoard it for yourself. This simple combination of ingredients seems to have been made specifically to be blended together. If you want to create a lighter dip you can reconstitute dehydrated sundried tomatoes in water instead of using oil packed ones. If this is your choice you will have to add at least a tablespoon of olive oil while mixing together the dip. There are also brands of light goat cheese which can be found in the deli section of some supermarkets which will also cut the fat and calories of this delectable dip.

Ingredients

2 cups oil packed sun-dried tomatoes, drained and chopped
2 ripe tomatoes, seeded and diced fine
1 cup soft goat cheese
1/2 cup minced scallions
1 tsp. minced garlic
Salt and pepper to taste
Fresh chopped basil

Method

1. Stir together sundried tomatoes, tomatoes, goat cheese, scallions and garlic until very well combined.
2. Season to taste and top with fresh basil. Place dip in the fridge for at least 6 hours up to 3 days.
3. Serve warm or cold with chips, vegetables, sliced baguette or pita bread.

Chili Peanut Dip

Peanuts are a very common delicious addition to stews, dips and sauces in North Africa and some Mediterranean cultures. This dip is hot, sweet, nutty, salty and slightly tart in a complex delicious combination that is perfect for barbecued meats and fresh cut vegetables. Peanuts often get a bad reputation as being too fatty and full of calories but they actually contain good fat (monounsaturated fat) and many healthy nutrients. Always be aware that peanuts can also cause life threatening allergic reactions in many people so to be safe only make this dip for events that do not have allergy sufferers in attendance. If you wish to create a healthier version of this delicious dip try using organic (no sugar added) peanut butter or even almond butter for an interesting taste variation.

Ingredients
1 cup smooth peanut butter
1/2 cup water
1/4 cup lime juice
1/4 cup brown sugar or honey
2 Tbsps. low sodium soy sauce
2 tsps. minced garlic
1 tsp. crushed chili flakes or to taste
1 tsp. chopped cilantro for garnish

Method
1. In a medium bowl whisk together all the ingredients and transfer to a serving dish. You can thin out the dip with a little more water if it is too thick.
2. Serve cold or hot with vegetables, crackers or spicy meat sates.

Loaded Baked Potato Dip

This dip can be paired up with French fries and potato chips or with toasted hollowed out roasted potato skins for the create a perfect loaded baked potato experience. It is not considered to be a healthy dip, it does contain bacon and cheese, but you can enjoy it every once in a while as a treat without too much guilt. You can reduce the amount of bacon and cheese as well as use light cream cheese but if you`re going to serve this comfort food you might as well present the tastiest unaltered version to your guests.

Ingredients
1 cup fat free sour cream
1 cup plain cream cheese
1/2 cup real bacon bits
1 cup shredded white cheddar cheese
1/4 cup chopped fresh chives
Salt and cracked black pepper to taste

Method
1. In a bowl beat together sour cream and cream cheese until very smooth.
2. Stir in bacon bits, cheese and most of the chives, reserving about a teaspoon of chives for garnish. Season to taste.
3. Chill in fridge until just before serving and then microwave dip until it is warmed through but not too hot.
4. Garnish with chives and serve with breads, chips or potato wedges.

Mediterranean Dip

Layered dips are lovely centerpieces for any event and have the added benefit of presenting complex ingredients conveniently stacked onto the chips or bread with no fuss or effort. People can just lift a chip and enjoy a combination of toppings. This dip features all the tastes associated with Mediterranean cuisines: ripe tomatoes, cool yogurt, toasty hummus and plump black olives. Olives are actually considered to be fruit and are packed with many antioxidant and anti-inflammatory nutrients. Olives are very good for the heart and the healthy Mediterranean diet includes this tasty ingredient as part of its meal plans. When making this delicious dip feel free to scatter a few extra olive slices on top or in between the other layers.

Ingredients
1 cup Greek yogurt
1 cup plain cream cheese, at room temperature
2 tsps. minced garlic
1 tsp. chopped fresh oregano
1/2 tsp. chopped fresh thyme
Salt and cracked black pepper to taste
Tortilla chips or toasted pita wedges
1 cup prepared Hummus
2 small plum tomatoes, seeded and diced
1 small cucumber, washed and diced, skin on
1 cup sliced Kalamata olives

Method
1. In a small bowl beat together the yogurt and cream cheese until very smooth. Beat in the garlic and herbs until well combined and season to taste. Set aside.
2. On a serving platter spread out the tortilla chips or pita wedges in a decorative manner. Spoon prepared hummus into the middle of the chips and spread it out as much as possible.
3. Spoon the yogurt mixture over the hummus and then top with diced cucumber, tomato and olives as evenly as possible.

Lemon Herb Cauliflower Bean Dip

If you don't mention to people that this dip is mostly cauliflower they will not realize it at all. Cauliflower is one of those lovely vegetables that seem to suck up the flavors and spices of the other ingredients while providing a nice meaty texture to the dish. Cauliflower is a member of the very healthy cruciferous vegetable family and should be included in your diet at least 3-4 times a week. This dip is a great way to get your fiber and nutrient packed serving without making it seem like a chore. If you want to change the recipe a little you can substitute just about any bean in this dip except perhaps black beans which would make the color an unappetizing grayish shade.

Ingredients

1 small head cauliflower, steamed or blanched until very tender
1 cup navy beans or chickpeas, rinsed and drained
3 Tbsps. tahini
1 tsp. minced garlic
2 Tbsps. extra virgin olive oil or as needed
Juice and zest of one lemon
1 Tbsp. chopped fresh thyme
Sea salt and fresh cracked pepper to taste
Fresh herb garnish

Method

1. Combine all ingredients in a food processor and pulse until well combined but not completely smooth.
2. Adjust seasoning and chill for at least 2 hours to allow flavors to develop.
3. Serve chilled or at room temperature with crackers, breads or fresh vegetables.

Creamy Cool Cucumber Dip

This recipe seems to be the epitome of spring. Cool, green and so fresh on the tongue you might want to top a salad with it instead of using it for a dip. This dip is much lower in fat than some other dips and can be further lightened by omitting the cream cheese. The coolness of cucumber dip is absolutely sublime when used for spicy meat skewers or even chicken wings because it seems to quench the heat of the spices. If you want a thicker dip you can allow your cucumber to drain in a colander before adding it to the other ingredients.

Ingredients

1 cup of fat free sour cream
1/4 cup plain light cream cheese, at room temperature
1 Tbsp. fresh lemon juice
1 Tbsp. granulated sugar
1 small cucumber, seeded and chopped finely
1/4 cup chopped fresh mint
Salt and pepper to taste
Mint sprigs for garnish

Method

1. In a large bowl whisk or beat together the sour cream and cream cheese until well combined and smooth.
2. Whisk in lemon juice and granulated sugar.
3. Stir in the chopped cucumber and mint. Season to taste.
4. Garnish with mint sprigs and serve with crackers, fresh cut vegetables and even with spicy meat skewers.

Cheesy Pizza Dip

Who doesn't like pizza with its dripping stretchy cheese and tasty tomato sauce? This dip takes that entire satisfying flavor combination and places it in one convenient bowl. The best part about this cheesy dip is you can enjoy it as is or add all your favorite pizza toppings right into the bowl. Some interesting additions could include chopped pepperoni, sautéed mushrooms and peppers, crumbled Italian sausage and even sliced olives. Another great feature of this dip is that you can store the finished dip in the fridge for up to a week and warm it up in the microwave for unexpected guests.

Ingredients

1 cup chopped sundried tomatoes
1 1/2 cups plain cream cheese, at room temperature
2 cups shredded mozzarella cheese
1/4 cup grated parmesan cheese
2 tsps. minced garlic
1/2 cup chopped fresh basil
2 Tbsps. chopped fresh thyme leaves
1 tsp. chopped fresh oregano leaves

Method

1. In a large saucepan mix together all ingredients over low heat until the mixture is melted and smooth.
2. Transfer cheese dip to a serving dish and serve with crackers, breads or chips.

BBQ Chicken Dip

Anyone who is a fan of bar style chicken wings will absolutely love this dip. It tastes almost identical to its on-the-bone counterparts and is less messy to eat. This dip uses lean chicken breast which is a great source of dietary protein, B vitamins, niacin and selenium. Make sure you use skinless chicken breasts for this recipe that are poached or roasted with very little oil so you don`t add too much extra fat to the end product. If you want to create a healthier version of the BBQ chicken dip reduce the amount of cream cheese and ranch dressing used and try low fat cheddar.

Ingredients

1 1/2 cups low fat cream cheese, at room temperature
1 cup prepared low fat ranch dressing
1/2 cup prepared barbeque sauce
1/2 cup shredded cheddar cheese
2 cups cooked shredded chicken breast
Splash of hot sauce (optional)

Method

1. Preheat the oven to 350 degrees F.
2. In a large bowl beat together the cream cheese, ranch dressing, barbecue sauce and cheese until very well combined.
3. Add hot sauce if using.
4. Stir in the shredded chicken until well mixed and transfer to a heat proof bowl.
5. Bake in the oven until dip is hot, about 15 minutes.
6. Serve with chips, crackers, breads or tortilla chips.

Chili Cheese Dip

This dip is a simplified version of chili con carne without the meat and need for a large stock pot. It is perfect for a Super Bowl party or casual family get together because although it isn`t elegant, it is flavor packed and filling. The beans add fiber and protein as well as a satisfying meatiness without the meat. Eating them on a regular basis can cut your risk of certain types of cancer, regulate your blood sugar and provide support for a healthy heart. If you want a very healthy version of this dip eliminate the shredded cheddar in the dip and only use a couple tablespoons to top it.

Ingredients

1 cup black beans
1 cup red kidney beans
1 cup puréed tomatoes
1 cup shredded cheddar
2 tsps. chili powder
1 tsp. cumin
Pinch cayenne
1/4 cup chopped fresh cilantro
1/2 cup shredded old cheddar
2 Tbsps. chopped scallion

Method

1. In a medium bowl mix together the beans, tomato, cheddar, chili powder, cumin, cayenne and cilantro. Adjust spicing and transfer to a heat proof bowl until you are ready to serve the dip.
2. Preheat oven to 350 degrees F. and top dip with shredded cheddar.
3. Heat in oven until dip is hot and the cheese is bubbly.
4. Top with green onions and serve.

Reuben Dip

This dip is unapologetically gooey, rich and yes, fattening but sometimes that is okay. It tastes like the classic sandwich and has all the aspects of the real Reuben; texture, melting cheese and a splash of hot sweet mustard. The best way to serve this dip is with big chunks of rye bread but it is also good with pita bread and tortilla chips. If you must make it healthier for your own piece of mind then use low fat cream cheese and cut the amounts of Swiss cheese and pastrami used for the dip.

Ingredients
1 pkg. (8 ounce) plain cream cheese, at room
temperature
1 cup shredded Swiss cheese
1 cup drained sauerkraut
1 cup finely chopped pastrami
1/2 cup sour cream
2 Tbsps. finely chopped sweet onion
2 Tbsps. hot mustard
4 thin slices Swiss cheese

Method
1. Preheat oven to 350 degrees F.
2. In a large bowl stir together all ingredients except cheese slices until well combined. You can add more mustard if you want it a little more spice.
3. Spray a 2-quart casserole dish lightly with cooking spray and spoon the dip mixture into the dish.
4. Top with cheese slices, overlapping them a little.
5. Bake in oven until bubbly, about 15 minutes.
6. Serve warm with rye bread chunks.

Artichoke Asiago Dip

dip is often found in the prepared foods section of the supermarket but it is easy to make an extremely delicious version at home as well. One of the benefits of making it at home is being able to control what goes into the dip and adjusting the seasoning to your own taste. Artichoke hearts are actually part of the head of a perennial thistle and a good source of antioxidants and fiber. If you have an issue with gallbladder disease you should avoid this dip because artichokes can stimulate gallbladder contraction.

Ingredients

1 1/2 cups artichoke hearts, drained and chopped
3/4 cup freshly shredded Asiago cheese
1 cup low fat mayonnaise
1/2 cup chopped scallion
1/2 tsp. minced garlic
Juice of 1 lemon
Sea salt and cracked black pepper to taste

Method

1. In a large bowl stir together all the ingredients until very well combined. Season to taste.
2. Transfer to a heat proof serving dish and refrigerate until you are ready to use the dip.
3. Heat in a 350 degree F. oven until dip is hot and bubbly.
4. Serve with breads or chips.

Spinach Dip

This is the staple dip in many homes, created with sour cream, mayo, frozen spinach and dry soup mix. This homemade version is lower in fat, creamier and has a stronger spinach flavor. Using fresh spinach also creates a brighter colored dip as long as you don`t blanch the spinach too long. Spinach is one of those lovely dark leafy greens recommended in most healthy eating plans because it has so many benefits. The list of nutrients and minerals contained in these pretty greens is extensive so include it whenever you can in salads, pastas and of course dips.

Ingredients

2 cups fresh spinach
2 cups light cream cheese
1/4 cup chopped scallions
2 Tbsps. minced carrot
2 Tbsps. minced sweet onion
2 Tbsps. chopped parsley
1/2 cup sour cream
Sea salt and cracked black pepper
1/4 cup shredded asiago cheese

Method

1. Steam or blanch spinach until it is tender, drain well and chop.
2. In a large bowl beat together the spinach, cream cheese, scallions, carrot, onion, sour cream and parsley until well combined.
3. Season to taste and transfer to heat proof serving dish topped with Asiago and refrigerate until you are ready to serve.
4. Heat in a 350 degree F. oven until dip is warmed through and cheese is bubbly.
5. Serve with chips, crackers, breads or tortilla chips.

Hot Seafood Dip

If you want an elegant subtle tasting dip to serve at a fancy party or business event this is a great choice to impress. This dip features a rich crab flavored base studded with gently curling delectable shrimp and pretty bits of scallion. There is a barely there taste of horseradish as well to round out the flavor profile. Horseradish goes beautifully with most seafood and whenever possible you should grate your own rather than buying prepared products. If you don`t use horseradish a great deal in your recipes then buy the prepared version because horseradish roots can be very large! Horseradish can stimulate the appetite and immune system, heat up the body and help control blood pressure.

Ingredients

2 cups plain low fat cream cheese, at room temperature
1/3 cup goat cheese, at room temperature
1 can crab meat or lobster, drained
1/3 cup baby shrimp, drained
2 Tbsps. chopped scallions
1 Tbsp. fresh lemon juice
1 Tbsp. fresh grated horseradish
Sea salt and pepper to taste
1 tsp. chopped fresh dill

Method

1. Combine all ingredients except dill in a large bowl, mixing well to combine. Season to taste.
2. Transfer to a baking pan and heat in a 300 degree F. oven until just warmed through.
3. Transfer to a serving bowl and garnish with dill.
4. Serve with crackers, chips, breads or tortillas.

Sweet Dips

Peanut Butter and Caramel Dip

This dip is absolutely perfect for an afterschool or mid-day snack with an assortment of apple wedges. It provides energy for kids dragged out from a busy day at school and will not be overly filling to spoil dinner. This dip will keep in the fridge for up to a week in a sealed container so feel free to double it for those times you need a quick sweet fix.

Ingredients
1 pkg. (8 ounces) plain low fat cream cheese at room temperature
3 tsps. golden brown sugar
3/4 cup smooth peanut butter
2 Tbsps. prepared caramel sauce
1 tsp. pure vanilla extract

Method
1. In a medium bowl using a hand mixer beat cream cheese until very smooth.
2. Add brown sugar and beat until smooth, scraping down the sides.
3. Add the rest of the ingredients and beat until completely smooth and creamy.
4. Place dip in the fridge until you are ready to use it. Take the dip out of the fridge about 15 minutes until it softens up a bit.
5. Serve with cut fruit, cookies, marshmallows or whatever you like.

Marshmallow Fruit Dip

Who wouldn't like to eat a dip that looks like a cloud and tastes like marshmallow cheesecake? This simple culinary creation melts in the mouth and combines beautifully with all fruits. If you can`t find a marshmallow fluff product then melt about 3 cups of mini marshmallows over very low heat and use that instead. Do not allow your melting marshmallows to brown up at all because it will ruin the pure white appearance of the dip.

Ingredients
1 pkg. (8 ounces) plain low fat cream cheese at room temperature
1 1/2 cups marshmallow fluff
1/2 cup confectioners' sugar
1/2 tsp. pure almond extract

Method
1. In a medium bowl beat cream cheese until completely smooth.
2. Add marshmallow fluff and beat until well combined.
3. Add confectioners' sugar and beat, scraping down the side of the bowl, until smooth.
4. Beat in almond extract.
5. Keep in fridge up to a week; serve with cut up fruit.

Cookie Dough Dip

There have been cakes, ice cream and candy created around the idea of chocolate chip cookie dough and countless prepared tubes of this popular product have been purchased with no intention of baking it into cookies. So why not create a dip that tastes the same but is thin enough to coat fruit or graham crackers? This dip is a little more complicated than most sweet dips and requires the use of a stove to melt some of the ingredients so make it ahead whenever possible. Take this dip out about 15 minutes before serving it so it softens up a little and makes dipping easier.

Ingredients
3/4 cup unsalted butter
1/2 cup golden brown sugar
1 Tbsp. pure vanilla extract
1 pkg. (8 ounce) plain cream cheese at room temperature
1/3 cup icing sugar
1 cup mini chocolate chips

Method
1. In a small saucepan over low heat combine butter, brown sugar and vanilla until brown sugar is dissolved and butter completely melted.
2. Remove from heat and set aside to cool.
3. In a medium bowl with a hand blender beat cream cheese until very smooth. Add confectioners' sugar and beat, scraping down the sides, until completely smooth.
4. Add butter mixture beating on low speed until fully incorporated and creamy.
5. Stir in the chocolate chips and transfer to a serving bowl.
6. Chill in fridge and serve with cut up fruit.

Brown Sugar Fruit Dip

This is a pretty dip that tastes a little like the melted brown sugar that you have on the top of a bowl of hot oatmeal but with a lighter fluffier texture! It will also definitely pick up the flavor of whatever liqueur you put in it; if you put any in the dip. This dip is very well matched with certain fruit including ripe black figs, peaches, nectarines, strawberries and mango. It will work with other fruit but those are sublime.

Ingredient

1 pkg. (8 ounces) plain low fat cream cheese, at room temperature
1 cup fat free sour cream
1/3 cup golden brown sugar, firmly packed
1 Tbsp. pure vanilla extract
1/4 cup chocolate or coffee liqueur (optional)
1/2 cup 35% heavy cream
4 Tbsps. toasted sliced almonds

Method

1. In a medium bowl with hand beaters beat cream cheese until very smooth. Add sour cream and beat, scraping down the sides of the bowl, until well combined.
2. Beat in the brown sugar, vanilla and liqueur until smooth and creamy.
3. In another medium bowl beat or whisk heavy cream until soft peaks form. Fold whipped cream into dip until smooth.
4. Transfer to a serving bowl, top with almonds and chill at least 4 hours before serving.

Toffee Cheesecake Dip

This dip is a fantasy come true for many people because it is like a cheesecake that can be dipped into with other delicious ingredients such as graham crackers and fruit. It is not necessarily healthy but it is fabulous for family events that are casual and festive. The spicing in this recipe can be adjusted to reflect your personal taste but the warm spices used in the original recipe are a perfect mix with the sweetness of the toffee bits. For a truly delicious variation you can chop up maple sugar and use that instead of the toffee.

Ingredients

1 pkg. (8 ounces) plain low fat cream cheese at room temperature
1/3 cup dark brown sugar
1/4 cup sour cream
1 Tbsp. pure vanilla extract
1/2 tsp. cinnamon
1/2 tsp. nutmeg
1/4 tsp. cloves
1/2 cup chopped Skor pieces or toffee baking bits

Method

1. In a medium bowl beat cream cheese until very smooth with hand beaters.
2. Add brown sugar and sour cream and beat until well combined.
3. Beat in vanilla, cinnamon, nutmeg and cloves, scraping down the sides, until smooth.
4. Stir in the toffee bits and chill until you are ready to use the dip.
5. Serve with fruit, cookies and marshmallows.

Apple Pie Dip

If a dip can represent fall, this apple topped beauty is autumn in a bowl. Apples can be purchased year round but they are usually naturally ripe in the crisp days of September, October and even November. Organic apples are a food you really should eat every day for good health because they pretty much contain all the nutrients you need in varying amounts within its pretty compact package. This dip could probably be used for fruit but it is really at its best with apple slices (yes, apple slices!), graham crackers, cinnamon sugar dusted tortilla chips and even baked pie crust cut into pretty shapes. It should be served at room temperature or warmer.

Ingredients

3 cups peeled, cored, and diced apple
2 Tbsps. fresh lemon juice
3 Tbsps. brown sugar
2 cups plain cream cheese, at room temperature
4 Tbsps. golden brown sugar
1 tsp. pure vanilla extract
1 tsp. cinnamon

Method

1. In a medium saucepan over medium low heat sauté apple with lemon juice and brown sugar until apple is cooked but not too soft.
2. Remove from heat and set aside.
3. In a medium bowl beat the cream cheese until smooth and fluffy and then beat in the brown sugar, vanilla and cinnamon.
4. Add about 11/2 cups of cooked apple to the cream cheese mixture and beat until mixture is very well combined but not smooth.
5. Spoon cream cheese mixture into a serving bowl and top with remaining cooked apple.
6. Serve with cookies, pieces of cooked pie crust or fruit slices.

Creamy Strawberry Dip

This is an extremely simple festive dip that is wonderful for children`s parties, baby showers and bridal showers. It is flavored with a sweet strawberry purée but you could use pretty much any berry depending on your personal preference. Strawberries are best when picked in season and they are an important addition to a healthy diet. They help boost immunity, support good eye health and help fight against several cancers. This dip should be set out for about 10 minutes before serving it so it is easier to scoop into with your cookies or fruit.

Ingredients
2 cups fresh strawberries, sliced
1/3 cup granulated sugar
1 cup plain low fat cream cheese or Neufchatel cheese,
at room temperature
1 cup sour cream

Method
1. In a small bowl over medium low heat stir together the strawberries and sugar until the berries start to purge liquid and sugar dissolves. Do not overcook or the berries will lose their fresh color.
2. Remove berries from heat and purée in a blender or with an immersion blender until smooth. Pass purée through a fine mesh sieve to remove the seeds.
3. In a medium bowl with hand beaters combine the cream cheese and sour cream until very smooth. Add the strawberry purée and beat until combined and fluffy.
4. Serve with fruit, marshmallows, chocolate and graham crackers.

Lemon Meringue Pie Dip

Lemons are an amazing fruit that stimulates several senses to create an exciting eating experience so this sunny dip should be served on cloudy days and during stressful times to boost the spirits. The brilliant color of the dip is enough to draw a smile, the scent can open your eyes and clear your mind, the flavor will make your taste buds snap and take notice. This dip is tart, sweet and incredibly buttery with no butter added! You can serve it with a fluffy meringue top or plain in a pretty crock surrounded by graham crackers and sugar cookies.

Ingredients
4 eggs, separated
1/2 cup fresh lemon juice
1 can sweetened condensed milk
1/4 cup granulated sugar
A dash of cream of tartar

Method
1. In a medium bowl placed over a saucepan of gently simmering water over low heat whisk together the egg yolks and lemon juice until thickened.
2. Place bowl in fridge covered with plastic wrap pressed right on the surface of the custard until cooled.
3. When custard is almost cool whisk together the egg whites and cream of tartar until soft peaks form. Add the sugar in tablespoons until you have a thick fluffy stiff peaked meringue.
4. Remove cooled custard from the fridge and whisk in the condensed milk.
5. If you aren't using the dip right away pour the custard into a jar and store in the fridge.
6. You can serve the dip as is if you aren't a fan of meringue. If you like meringue, place the lemon custard in a serving bowl and heap the meringue on top by tablespoons.
7. Place the bowl under a broiler for a few minutes until browned. Serve with graham crackers, fruit or anything else that strikes your fancy!

ONE LAST THING

We would love to get your feedback about our book:

If you enjoyed this book or found it useful, we would be very grateful if you would post a short review on Amazon. Your support really does make a difference and we read all of the reviews personally, so we can get your feedback and make our books even better.

If you would like to leave a review, all you need to do is click the review link on this book's page on Amazon

Thank you again for your support!

Sign up for free ebooks

Echo Bay Books is proud to bring you our latest and greatest eBooks on Amazon. We treat you as a guest, and we treat our guests well. We promise to only send you notifications if it has some goodies attached that we think you will like. We launch our eBooks for free for the first 5 days every time. That means you will be the first to know when new books launch (once per week) - for FREE. No spam, ever. Just go to
http://bit.ly/1bMhUhf
 to start receiving your free ebooks!

EXCERPT FROM "MUFFIN TIN MEALS RECIPES"

What Are Muffin Tin Meals?

Muffin tin meals are any food that is prepared in a muffin tin instead of a traditional pan, dish, or tray. A muffin tin meal can be breakfast, lunch, dinner, dessert, or a side dish baked straight in a muffin pan.

They're easy, perfect portions that are fun and different to eat. Muffin tin meals are mess-free, too -- there's no cutting of servings required, and they freeze in perfect amounts. Once you start cooking in muffin tins you'll be hooked!

From Concept To Creation: Making Your Own Muffin Tin Meals

Want to try out your own muffin tin meals? We've provided 20 easy recipes for every meal in this book. But if you get eager to try more, you're in luck -- many recipes can be adapted to work in muffin tins. It usually comes down to just spooning the ingredients into a lined or greased muffin tin instead of a baking pan. Once you've become comfortable making these recipes, you'll find it is much easier to adapt your family's favorites into muffin tin portions.

You can already customize many of the meals in this book by leaving out ingredients, like veggies, meats and cheese, or switching them up to suit your tastes. Since every muffin cup is individual, it's easy to leave out ingredients you don't like, and add ones that you do. You can also experiment with half batches to try new meals and experiment with flavors.

There are a few rules and guidelines to follow when baking in muffin tins to get the best results. The main rule is to fill each cup 2/3 full to avoid spilling and burnt tops. Also remember to watch the timer closely – since muffin trays can be different sizes, and oven temperatures can vary, you'll want to keep an eye on your muffin tin meals as the timer nears the end of the bake time.

Aside from that, muffin tin meals are all about having fun and creating easy-to-eat portions, so get in the kitchen and try out some recipes!

Chicken and Broccoli Cups

Yields 12

Ingredients

2 cups cooked chicken, diced
1 can cream of chicken soup
1 cup broccoli, diced
1 garlic clove, minced
salt and pepper, to taste
Premade biscuit dough
1/4 cup grated Parmesan cheese (optional)

Method

Preheat oven to 375F and grease a standard muffin tin.

Combine the first five ingredients, tossing to mix well. Press the biscuit dough into the muffin tins, contouring to the sides of the pan. Spoon the chicken mixture into the dough cups, and sprinkle with the cheese.

Bake for 20-30 minutes, until golden brown.

Nutritional Info

Calories 79
Fat 3.0g
Total Carbohydrates 4.6g
Protein 8.0g

CONNECT WITH US ON OUR SPECIAL FACEBOOK PAGE

Come join our Facebook page to be the first to hear when the next book in the Easy Recipe series is released. On this page, we will also share bonus content for you to enjoy.

It's also a great place to get any questions you have answered as well.

Come join us here on Facebook:

http://facebook.com/echobaybooks

10009398R00054

Printed in Great Britain
by Amazon.co.uk, Ltd.,
Marston Gate.